Somewhere
in the
Universe

David Drew

**Illustrations by
Dorothy Dunphy and
Donna Rawlins**

**Maps by
Neil Kennan**

Somewhere in the universe
is our galaxy.
It's called the Milky Way.
Can you find it?

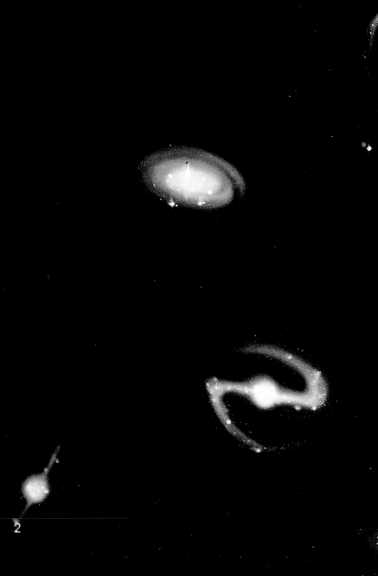

The Milky Way

Somewhere in the Milky Way
is our Solar System.
It has one Sun and
nine planets.
Can you find it?

planets

Solar System

prominence

Sun

sunspot

Somewhere in our Solar System
is the Earth.
It's a small, blue planet.
Can you find it?

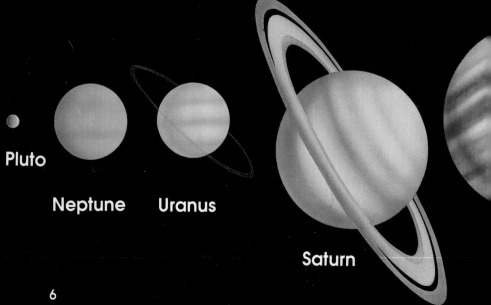

Pluto

Neptune   Uranus

Saturn

Sun

Mars　Earth　Venus　Mercury

Jupiter

Can you find it on the map?

Somewhere in our country is the state we live in. Can you find it?

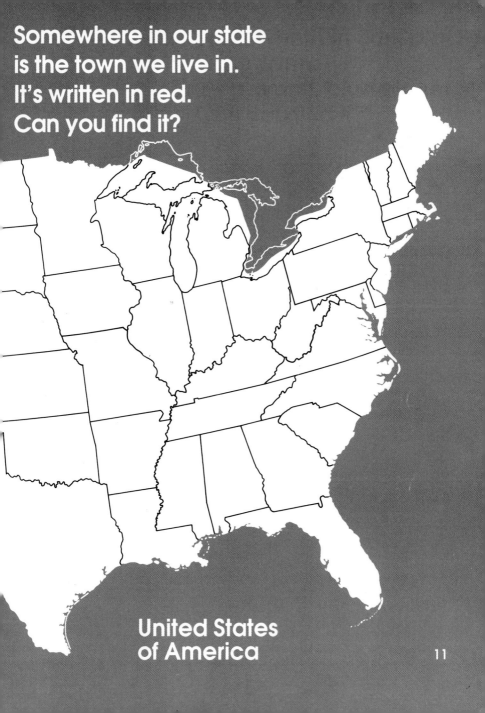

Somewhere in our state
is the town we live in.
It's written in red.
Can you find it?

United States
of America

Somewhere in our town
is the street Jason lives on.
It's the street beside the park.
Can you find it?

Can you find it on the map?

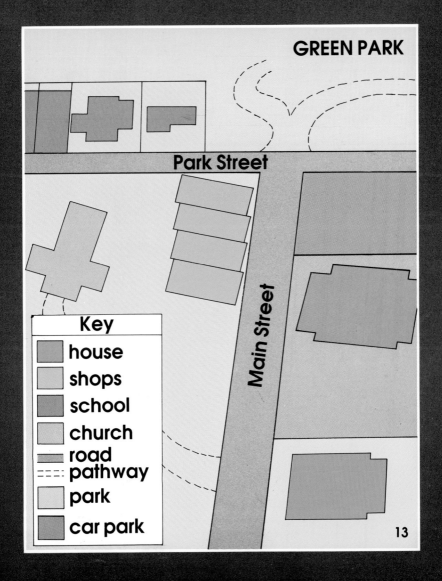

GREEN PARK

Park Street

Main Street

Key

- house
- shops
- school
- church
- road
- - - - pathway
- park
- car park

13

Somewhere on Jason's street
is his house.
It's the house with
grass in front of it.
Can you find it?

Somewhere on the grass
is Jason.
He's hiding behind the bushes.
Can you find him?

Here he is!